Smithsonian

DIGGING FOR STEGOSAURUS

BY THOMAS R. HOLTZ JR., Ph.D.

A Discovery TIMELINE

CAPSTONE PRESS
a capstone imprint

Capstone Press
1710 Roe Crest Drive
North Mankato, Minnesota 56003
www.capstonepub.com

The name of the Smithsonian Institution and the sunburst logo
are registered trademarks of the Smithsonian Institution.
For more information, please visit www.si.edu.

Our very special thanks to Mike Brett-Surman, PhD, Museum Specialist for
Fossil Dinosaurs, Reptiles, Amphibians, and Fish at the National Museum of
Natural History, Smithsonian Institution, for his curatorial review. Capstone would
also like to thank Kealy Wilson, Product Development Manager, and the following
at Smithsonian Enterprises: Ellen Nanney, Licensing Manager; Brigid Ferraro,
Vice President, Education and Consumer Products; Carol LeBlanc,
Senior Vice President, Education and Consumer Products.

Editorial Credits

Kristen Mohn, editor; Lori Bye and Aruna Rangarajan, designers;
Kelly Garvin, media researcher; Kathy McColley, production specialist

Photo Credits

AP Images/Ed Andrieski, 26(top right); Corbis: Lake County Museum, 5, Louie
Psihoyos, 17(bottom), 18(bottom left): Dreamstime: Vaclav Volrab, 11(bottom
right); Getty Images: Andrew Bret Wallis, 18(tr), De Agostini Picture Library,
25(br), Hulton Archive, 7(bl), Karl Gehring, 14(tr), Kathryn Scott Osler, 15; Jon
Hughes, cover, 7(tr), 16, 19, 20(tr), 27(top), 29; Library of Congress/Prints &
Photographs Division, 9(tr); Newscom/Peter Bennett, 23; Photo courtesy of Bruce
Rothschild, 22(bottom); Photo courtesy of Don Pfister, PaleoGallery.com 26(b);
Photo courtesy of Miriam Reichel taken by Scott Persons, 27(br); Photo courtesy
of Octavio Mateus, 24(bl); 24-25(t); Royal Gorge Regional Museum & History
Center, 9(bl), 20(b); Science Source: 14(bl), Paul D. Stewart, 6(bl); Scientific
American, 8(b), Shutterstock: Catmando, backcover, 1, damair, 12(tr); Wikimedia:
Benjamin Waterhouse Hawkins, 6(tr), 9(tl), Ayca Wilson, 17(t), Charles Gilmore,
10(b), Charles Knight, 11(t), Frank Bond, 8(t), Frederick Berger, 12(bl),
FunkMonk, 21, Hetmanber, 13, Kevmin, 22(tr), Popular Science Monthly,
11(bl), Othniel C. Marsh, 10(tr)

Library of Congress Cataloging-in-Publication Data

Holtz, Thomas R., 1965– author.
Digging for stegosaurus: a discovery timeline / by Thomas R. Holtz, Jr.
pages cm. —(Smithsonian. Dinosaur discovery timelines)
Summary: "Provides an annotated timeline of the discovery of Stegosaurus
including details on the scientists, dig sites, fossils, and other findings that have
shaped our knowledge of this dinosaur"—Provided by publisher.
Audience: Ages 8–12.
Audience: Grade 2–6.
Includes bibliographical references and index.
ISBN 978-1-4914-2124-6 (library binding)
ISBN 978-1-4914-2365-3 (paperback)
1. Stegosaurus—Juvenile literature. 2. Paleontology—Juvenile literature.
[1. Dinosaurs.] I. Title.
QE862.O65H663 2015
567.915'3—dc23   2014031830

Printed in Canada.
092014   008478FRS15

Table of Contents

STEGOSAURUS

Stegosaurus was one of the strangest-looking dinosaurs. It had a small, beaked head and a very big body. Flat bones called plates stuck up along its back. Four spikes jutted out from the end of its tail. Even people who know very little about dinosaurs recognize *Stegosaurus*.

No humans lived during the time of *Stegosaurus*, so how do we know about this creature? We know about it because scientists have found and studied its fossils. Fossils are bones, teeth, footprints, and other remains that are preserved in rocks. Paleontologists—people who study fossils—use these remains to piece together the lives and habits of ancient creatures.

Usually, paleontologists don't start with a complete skeleton of a dinosaur. Instead, they study the animal rock by rock, bone by bone. And this is how we learned about *Stegosaurus*. Here is the story of the discoveries that helped us understand this ancient armored beast.

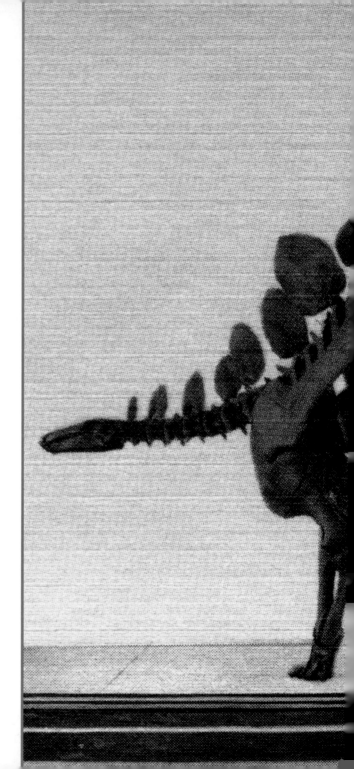

Tilgate Forest and Swindon, United Kingdom:
The Discovery of Armored Dinosaurs

Hylaeosaurus

November 1832
Mantell names the fossil *Hylaeosaurus* ("forest lizard"). He realizes that some of the bones were actually armored spikes.

July 1832
Quarry workers in Tilgate Forest find a partial skeleton in rocks. Paleontologist Gideon Mantell buys the bones. He believes the bones are from the shoulder area and part of the back of some kind of reptile.

1842
Sir Richard Owen, Britain's chief paleontologist, assigns the name Dinosauria to an extinct group of giant reptiles. His original three types of dinosaurs are meat-eating *Megalosaurus*, plant-eating *Iguanodon*, and armored *Hylaeosaurus*.

Dacentrurus

1902
Frederic Augustus Lucas, another paleontologist, gives the Swindon dinosaur a new name: *Dacentrurus* ("tail full of points"). Many additional *Dacentrurus* fossils had been found, but none were complete.

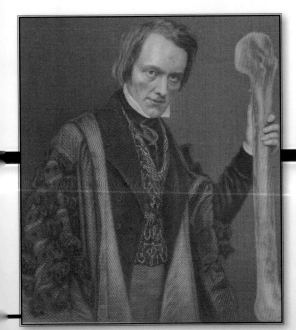

1874
Miner James Shopland finds part of a skeleton in a clay pit in Swindon. Owen identifies it as a dinosaur. The skeleton includes a few armor plates and spikes.

1875
Owen names the Swindon dinosaur *Omosaurus* ("upper arm lizard"). He does not realize that name has already been given to another fossil reptile.

7

Morrison and Garden Park, Colorado; and Como Bluff, Wyoming: *The Shingled Reptile*

1914 drawing shows plates lying flat and spikes all over back

November 15, 1877
Marsh publishes a description of the Morrison fossil. He is not certain it is a dinosaur, because he sees similarities in it to sea reptiles and turtles. Because the skeleton is incomplete and has fallen apart, he does not know what to do with its armor plates. He figures that the plates were stacked like roof shingles on the reptile's back, so he names it *Stegosaurus* ("shingled lizard"). At this point Marsh thinks *Stegosaurus* moved mainly by swimming.

Summer 1877
Geologist and fossil hunter Arthur Lakes and engineer H. C. Beckwith are looking for fossils for paleontologist Othniel Charles Marsh. They find the skeleton of a large reptile near the town of Morrison, Colorado.

Arthur Lakes' sketch of the fossils found near Morrison

1879
At Como Bluff, fossil hunters Arthur Lakes and William Reed discover a new *Stegosaurus* skeleton. It is much more complete than the earlier finds. The Como Bluff skeleton shows Marsh that *Stegosaurus* is a dinosaur and not a sea reptile, that it is the same type of dinosaur that Cope called *Hypsirhophus*, and that it had spikes on its tail.

1878
Fossil hunter Oramel W. Lucas is working in Garden Park for paleontologist Edward Drinker Cope. He finds a very incomplete skeleton. Recognizing it as a dinosaur, Cope names it *Hypsirhophus* ("high roof") because of its tall backbones.

Garden Park dig site

EXPERTS: *Edward Drinker Cope, Othniel Charles Marsh,* and the Bone War

Edward Drinker Cope (1840–1897) and Othniel Charles Marsh (1831–1899) were two of the most important paleontologists of all time. Both made many important discoveries of dinosaurs and other ancient animals. Cope and Marsh are famous for their great rivalry, nicknamed the Bone War.

Cope and Marsh started off as friends, but they were jealous of each other's discoveries. Each wanted to make bigger and better discoveries than the other. When the first good fossilized skeletons of dinosaurs and mammals were discovered in the western United States, Cope and Marsh each sent out teams to hunt for skeletons. Their crews spied on each other to learn about their finds. They also tried to make deals with landowners to be the only crew with rights to look for fossils in certain areas. They sometimes even smashed bones if they thought the other team might dig them out first!

This kind of rivalry was mostly harmful, but in some ways the competition was good. Marsh and Cope made many important discoveries in a short period of time. They found the first complete dinosaur fossils, and the world began to learn what dinosaurs looked like. These fossils became displays at museums. Now the public could see these ancient bones for themselves.

Como Bluff, Wyoming, and Garden Park, Colorado:
A Complete Stegosaurus: The Plate Puzzle

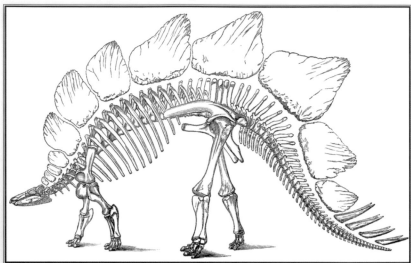

Marsh's 1896 illustration of *Stegosaurus*

1879
William Reed and his worker E. G. Ashley find many nearly complete dinosaur fossils in a layer of rock at Como Bluff. For many more years, Reed and his team will dig dinosaurs from this quarry for Marsh.

1885
Fossil hunter Marshall P. Felch finds a nearly complete *Stegosaurus* at Garden Park. Until the 1990s this will be the most complete *Stegosaurus* fossil known.

1891
Marsh theorizes that *Stegosaurus'* big, flat plates are arranged in a single row down its back.

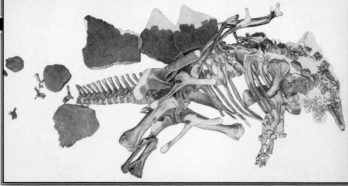

Stegosaurus fossils

Stegosaurus painting showing plates in pairs

1914
Smithsonian paleontologist Charles W. Gilmore studies Felch's skeleton in great detail. He decides that the plates were most likely arranged in two rows down the back. However, the plates alternate between one side and the other instead of being next to each other in pairs.

1901
Frederic Lucas of the Smithsonian Institution in Washington, D.C., suggests that *Stegosaurus'* plates are arranged in pairs down its back.

Stegosaurus with alternating plates

Frederic Augustus Lucas

Como Bluff, Wyoming: *Tiny Heads and "Bottom Brains"?*

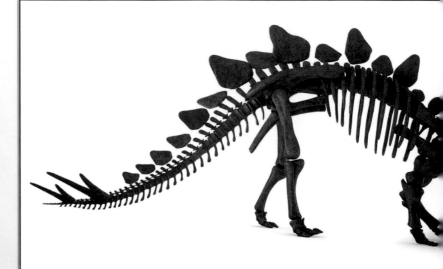

1880
Marsh examines and describes the best *Stegosaurus* skull found so far. He is amazed by how small the space for the brain is. He states, correctly, that compared to its body size, *Stegosaurus* has the smallest brain of all known animals at the time.

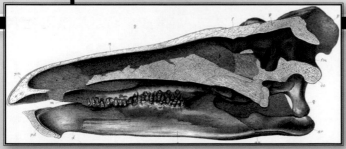

Stegosaurus brain cavity shown in red

February 1881
Marsh continues to describe the Como Bluff specimens. He finds a space in the animal's hips. He guesses that this space held a very large amount of nerves. Basically, he says, *Stegosaurus* had a brain in its rear end! (Marsh had the same idea about the dinosaur *Camarasaurus* in 1879.)

Stegosaurus skull

March 1881
A scientist, writing under the initials B. G. W., states that *Stegosaurus'* hip space was not for a brain; more likely it held other tissue. Even so, the idea of a second brain remains popular with the public for nearly a century.

1991
Paleontologist Emily Giffin shows that the hip space was not for extra nerves, but for fatty tissue. It was not a "butt brain" at all.

Como Bluff, Wyoming: *Two Legs or Four?*

Robert Bakker

1880
Marsh sees the Como Bluff skeleton and finds that the front legs are much shorter than the back legs. He guesses that *Stegosaurus* walked on just two legs.

1891
Marsh looks at better specimens. He is now convinced that *Stegosaurus* walked on all fours but that perhaps it could rear up on its hind legs to feed higher in trees.

1986
Paleontologist Robert T. Bakker looks at newer fossils and agrees with Marsh's 1891 idea about rearing. He bases this on where the dinosaur's point of balance would be.

an early interpretation of *Stegosaurus*

1998
Paleontologist Kenneth Carpenter disagrees with Marsh and Bakker. When he looks at the back plates, he concludes that *Stegosaurus* wouldn't have been able to bend properly to stand on its back legs.

2010
Using computer models of skeletons, paleontologist Heinrich Mallison shows that rearing would have been possible for some plated dinosaurs, perhaps including *Stegosaurus*.

Tendaguru Hill, Tanzania, and Zigong, China: *Cousins in Other Lands*

1915
German paleontologist Edwin Hennig names the African stegosaur *Kentrosaurus* ("sharp point lizard"). *Kentrosaurus* was smaller than *Stegosaurus*, had smaller and fewer plates, and had more and longer spikes.

1909
At a major dinosaur dig in the area that later becomes Tanzania, workers find the remains of a *Stegosaurus*-like plated dinosaur. In the next few years, hundreds of bones will be uncovered.

Kentrosaurus

Tuojiangosaurus mounted at the Natural History Museum in London

1974
Workers building the Wujiaba Dam in Zigong find the bones of a dinosaur.

1977
China's chief paleontologist, Dong Zhiming, and colleagues name the new dinosaur *Tuojiangosaurus*, after the Tuo River. (Jiang is "river" in Chinese.) Like *Stegosaurus*, *Tuojiangosaurus* has only a few tail spikes. However, its plates are more triangular and pointed than those of *Kentrosaurus* and *Stegosaurus*.

1982
Not far from the *Tuojiangosaurus* digging site, workers find partial skeletons of 12 other plated dinosaurs. They are of a different, earlier kind, which Dong and colleagues named *Huayangosaurus*, after the province where they were discovered.

Dong Zhiming

Como Bluff, Wyoming: *What Are the Plates For?*

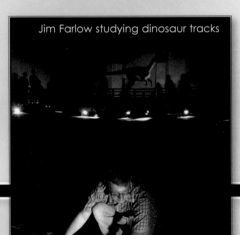

Jim Farlow studying dinosaur tracks

1998
Ken Carpenter has other ideas. He thinks *Stegosauruses* used their plates to recognize each other, and also to stiffen and support the back.

1976
Paleontologist James Farlow and colleagues challenge the theory that *Stegosaurus* used its plates only for defense. Farlow's simple model shows that the reptile might have used its plates to shed heat if it got too hot, or to warm up if it got too cold.

2005
Biologist Russell Main and some paleontologist colleagues look at the internal structure of *Stegosaurus* plates. These scientists find that the plates probably would not have been good for losing or gaining heat.

2010
Farlow combines Main's information with new data from other *Stegosaurus* plates and from the armor of modern alligators. He shows that the big plates could have lost and gained heat as a side effect. However, the plates' main functions were to act as armor and to help the animal show off.

Garden Park, Colorado: *The Thagomizer*

1992
At Garden Park, paleontologist Bryan Small finds a *Stegosaurus* skeleton. He and colleagues Tim Seeber and Ken Carpenter uncover the specimen. It is one of the most complete stegosaurs ever found. It gets the nickname "Spike."

1982
Gary Larson, creator of the comic strip *The Far Side*, publishes a cartoon in which a caveman talks to a friend about *Stegosaurus*. (In reality, no caveman ever met a living *Stegosaurus*!) The caveman calls the spiky end of the dinosaur's tail a "thagomizer." (He names the tail after the late caveman Thag Simmons, who must have been killed by one.)

Chinook helicopter lifting the 7-ton (6.4 metric ton) plastered fossil

1993
Carpenter describes Spike at a meeting in New Mexico. Using Larson's nickname, he calls the spiky tail a "thagomizer." Carpenter shows that the spikes stuck out to the side, not straight up as most paleontologists had thought.

Kentrosaurus tail on display in Berlin, Germany

1998
Carpenter suggests that the overlapping plates of *Stegosaurus'* tail meant it could not whip its tail from side to side very well.

2011
Heinrich Mallison creates a computer model for the tail of *Kentrosaurus*. The model shows that this dinosaur's tail could swing from side to side quite a bit. Mallison argues that *Stegosaurus'* tail could do the same.

Garden Park, Colorado, and Cleveland-Lloyd Dinosaur Quarry, Utah: *Stegosaurus Defense*

Stegosaurus tail spikes on display at the Denver Museum of Nature and Science

1998
Carpenter notes that two of Spike's thagomizer spikes were damaged while the dinosaur was alive.

Bruce Rothschild

2001
Bruce Rothschild, an expert on fossil injuries and illnesses, studies Spike and other *Stegosaurus* fossils with his colleagues. They find that 1 out of every 10 thagomizer spikes was damaged. Most often their tips had broken off.

2005

Carpenter and colleagues show that some bones of *Allosaurus* (the main meat eater from the same environment as *Stegosaurus*), which were found at Cleveland-Lloyd Quarry, were damaged by thagomizer spikes. The bones also show that *Stegosaurus* plates from the same quarry have bite marks that match the shape of *Allosaurus* jaws. Scientists now have proof that *Allosaurus* and *Stegosaurus* fought.

Miragaia, Portugal: *A Long-Necked Portuguese Cousin*

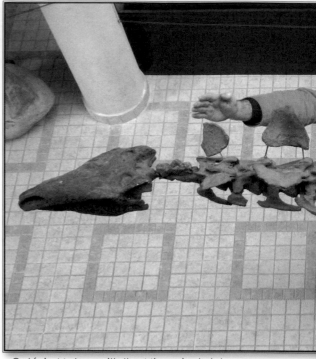

Octávio Mateus with the *Miragaia* skeleton

1999
A construction crew finds dinosaur bones while building a road between the villages of Miragaia and Sobral in Portugal.

Miragaia excavation in Portugal

2001
The Portugal skeleton is now completely collected. It is the entire front half of a plated dinosaur.

2010
Paleontologist Alberto Cobos and colleagues state that the features that Mateus used to conclude that *Miragaia* is a brand-new dinosaur are all in parts of the body that haven't yet been found for *Dacentrurus*. Thus, the Portuguese dinosaur may be a *Dacentrurus* instead of a new type of dinosaur.

2009
Paleontologist Octávio Mateus and colleagues describe this fossil as a brand-new type of plated dinosaur. They name it *Miragaia* after the nearby town. Unlike most stegosaurs, it has a very long neck. There are more vertebrae in its neck (17) than in *Stegosaurus'* (13).

Dacentrurus

Shell, Wyoming, and Morrison, Colorado: *New Discoveries*

Matthew Mossbrucker

2005
Paleontologist Matthew Mossbrucker finds the first baby *Stegosaurus* footprints in Morrison, Colorado, not far from where Arthur Lakes found the first *Stegosaurus*.

2004
Fossil hunter Bob Simon finds a nearly complete skeleton of *Stegosaurus* in Shell. They nickname it Sarah in honor of the local rancher's daughter.

Bob Simon on a dig at the Morrison Formation

2010
Paleontologist Miriam Reichel studies Sarah and other *Stegosaurus* specimens with well-preserved skulls. She calculates that *Stegosaurus* had a very weak bite—not much stronger than the bite of a Labrador dog—even though it was a much bigger animal.

2008
Mossbrucker's study of the tracks shows that *Stegosaurus* probably lived in groups.

Miriam Reichel

About *Stegosaurus*

Length: up to 30 feet (9 meters)

Height: up to 13 feet (4 m) or more at the top of the plates

Weight: 5 tons (4.5 metric tons) or possibly more

Age: lived 156 to 147 million years ago, in the later part of the Jurassic Period

Location: Western North America

Diet: soft plants that grow low to the ground

Distinctive features: Seventeen vertical broad plates, starting at the neck and running to the tail. Four spikes form a "thagomizer" weapon on the tail. A very small head with a beak.

Enemies: *Allosaurus*, *Torvosaurus*, and *Ceratosaurus* were the main enemies for an adult *Stegosaurus*. Babies would have to look out for various small meat eaters.

Relatives: *Tuojiangosaurus* of China, *Kentrosaurus* of Tanzania, *Dacentrurus* of England, and *Miragaia* of Portugal

Fighting: Swiping the "thagomizer" spikes would be one type of protection. The plates were probably not helpful as armor, but they made *Stegosaurus* look bigger.

Glossary

fossil—the remains of a living thing (like bones and teeth) or traces of its action (like footprints) preserved in the rock record; evidence of life from the geologic past

geologist—a scientist who studies minerals, rocks, and soil

Jurassic Period—the span of geologic time from 200 to 145 million years ago; the second of three geologic periods from the Mesozoic Era

paleontologist—a scientist who studies fossils

plate—a flat bone that sticks up out of the back of *Stegosaurus* or its relatives

quarry—a place where stone or other minerals are dug from the ground

rival—a person or thing that tries to outdo or be better than another person or thing

specimen—a particular individual or sample of something; in fossils, a specimen is the remains of one particular example of a species

spike—a cone-shaped bone that sticks out of the side of the tail of *Stegosaurus* or its relatives

thagomizer—the spiky tail weapon of *Stegosaurus* and its relatives

theorize—to form a theory or an educated guess

theory—an idea that explains something that is unknown

tissue—a layer or bunch of soft material that makes up body parts

vertebra—a back bone; more than one vertebra are vertebrae

Read More

Bakker, Robert T., and Luis V. Rey (illus.). *The Big Golden Book of Dinosaurs*. New York: Golden Book, 2013.

Brusatte, Steve. *Field Guide to Dinosaurs*. New York: Book Sales Inc., 2009.

Holtz Jr., Thomas R. *Dinosaurs: The Most Complete, Up-to-Date Encyclopedia for Dinosaur Lovers of All Ages*. New York: Random House, 2007.

McCurry, Kristen, and Juan Calle (illus.). *How to Draw Incredible Dinosaurs*. North Mankato, Minn.: Capstone Press, 2013.

Internet Sites

Use FactHound to find Internet sites related to this book. All of the sites on FactHound have been researched by our staff.

Here's all you do:

Visit www.facthound.com

Type in this code: 9781491421246

ABOUT THE AUTHOR

Thomas R. Holtz Jr. is a vertebrate paleontologist with the University of Maryland Department of Geology. He has authored dozens of books and articles on dinosaurs for children and adults. He has even appeared in dinosaur-themed comic strips. A graduate of Yale and Johns Hopkins, Dr. Holtz lives in Maryland when he's not traveling the world, hunting fossils.

Index

Bibliography

Carpenter, K. 1998. Armor of Stegosaurus stenops, and the taphonomic history of a new specimen from Garden Park, Colorado. Modern Geology 22: 127–44.

Carpenter, K. (ed.). 2001. The Armored Dinosaurs. Indiana University Press. 512 pp.

Carpenter K., F. Sanders, L. McWhinney & L. Wood. Evidence for predator-prey relationships: examples for Allosaurus and Stegosaurus. Pp. 325–350, in Carpenter, K. (ed.), The Carnivorous Dinosaurs. Indiana University Press.

Farlow, J.O., C.V. Thompson & D.E. Rosner. 1976. Plates of the dinosaur Stegosaurus: forced convection heat loss fins? Science 192: 1123–1125. doi:10.1126/science.192.4244.1123.

Gilmore, C.W. 1914. Osteology of the armored Dinosauria in the United States National Museum, with special reference to the genus Stegosaurus. Bulletin of the US National Museum 89: 1–136.

Giffin, E.B. 1990. Gross spinal anatomy and limb use in living and fossil reptiles. Paleobiology 16: 448–458.

Main, R., A. de Ricqlès, J. Horner & K. Padian. 2005. The evolution and function of thyreophoran dinosaur scutes: implications for plate function in stegosaurs. Paleobiology 31: 291–314. Doi: 10.1666/0094-8373(2005)031[0291:TEAFOT]2.0.CO;2.

Marsh, O.C. 1877. A new order of extinct Reptilia (Stegosauria) from the Jurassic of the Rocky Mountains. American Journal of Science 3: 513–514.

Mallison, H. 2011. Defense capabilities of Kentrosaurus aethiopicus Hennig, 1915 Palaeontogia Electronica 14.2.10A.

Mateus, O., S.C.R. Maidment & N.A. Christiansen. 2009. A new long-necked 'sauropod-mimic' stegosaur and the evolution of the plated dinosaurs. Proceedings of the Royal Society B: Biological Sciences 276: 1815–1821. doi:10.1098/rspb.2008.1909.

Naish, D. & D.M. Martill. 2008. Dinosaurs of Great Britain and the role of the Geological Society of London in their discovery: Ornithischia. Journal of the Geological Society, London 165: 613–623. doi: 10.1144/0016-76492007-154.

Reichel, M. 2010. A model for the bite mechanics in the herbivorous dinosaur Stegosaurus (Ornithischia, Stegosauridae). Swiss Journal of Geosciences 103: 235–240. Doi: 10.1007/s00015-010-0025-1.